T0413865

HIPPOPOTAMUS

By Colleen Sexton

BEARPORT
PUBLISHING

Minneapolis, Minnesota

Credits:

Cover and title page, © andyKRAKOVSKI/iStock; 3, © Ingrid Heres/Shutterstock; 4–5, © slowmotiongli/iStock; 6, © komkrit Preechachanwate/Shutterstock; 7, © Christiane Schwerin/Shutterstock; 8, © slowmotiongli/iStock; 9, © Phillip Allaway/Shutterstock; 10, © undefined undefined/iStock; 11, © Robby_Holmwood/iStock; 13, © nwdph/Shutterstock; 14, © Jaynes Gallery / DanitaDelimont/Alamy; 15, © Aida Servi/Shutterstock; 16–17, © Mark Boulton/Alamy; 19, © Goddard_Photography/iStock; 20–21, © Vaclav Sebek/Shutterstock; 22L, © Silbervogel/Shutterstock; 22R, © Car n food designer/Shutterstock; and 23, © LouisLotterPhotography/Shutterstock.

Bearport Publishing Company Product Development Team
President: Jen Jenson; Director of Product Development: Spencer Brinker; Senior Editor: Allison Juda; Editor: Charly Haley; Associate Editor: Naomi Reich; Senior Designer: Colin O'Dea; Associate Designer: Elena Klinkner; Product Development Assistant: Anita Stasson

Library of Congress Cataloging-in-Publication Data

Names: Sexton, Colleen A., 1967- author.
Title: Hippopotamus / by Colleen Sexton.
Description: Minneapolis, Minnesota : Bearport Publishing Company, [2023] | Series: Library of awesome animals | Includes bibliographical references and index.
Identifiers: LCCN 2021061874 (print) | LCCN 2021061875 (ebook) | ISBN 9798885091091 (library binding) | ISBN 9798885091169 (pcperback) | ISBN 9798885091237 (ebook)
Subjects: LCSH: Hippopotamidae--Juvenile literature.
Classification: LCC QL737.U57 S49 2023 (print) | LCC QL737.U57 (ebook) | DDC 599.63/5--dc23/eng/20211222
LC record available at https://lccn.loc.gov/2021061874
LC ebook record available at https://lccn.loc.gov/2021061875

For more information, write to Bearport Publishing, 5357 Penn Avenue South, Minneapolis, MN 55419. Printed in the United States of America.

Contents

AWESOME
Hippopotamuses!

SPLASH! A huge hippopotamus rushes into a river. From their giant mouths to their bulky bodies, hippos are awesome!

HIPPOPOTAMUSES SPEND TIME IN WATER AND ON LAND. THEIR NAME MEANS RIVER HORSE IN GREEK.

These chunky animals are known for their round, barrel-shaped bodies. They hold themselves up on four short legs, with **hooves** protecting four toes on each foot. Thick skin keeps the rest of their bodies safe, from their big heads to their small, flat tails.

A HIPPO SWEATS ITS OWN SUNSCREEN. THIS RED SWEAT LOOKS A LOT LIKE BLOOD!

Twice as Nice

There are two kinds of hippos, and both call Africa home. Common hippos are bigger. They have bulging eyes, large **nostrils**, and round ears on top of their heads. Their **webbed** toes help them move through the rivers and lakes near where they live.

Pygmy hippos spend more time in forests. Longer legs and spaces between their toes help these smaller hippos walk in mud.

Pygmy hippo

COMMON HIPPOS ARE AMONG THE WORLD'S LARGEST LAND ANIMALS, ALONG WITH ELEPHANTS AND RHINOS.

Common hippos

9

In the Water

Hippos spend their days resting and sleeping. They lie in mud or stand in water to stay cool. In water, hippos often keep their eyes, ears, and noses above the surface. But sometimes, they close their nostrils and sink! These amazing animals can hold their breath underwater for up to five minutes. **WOW!**

HIPPOS CAN EVEN SLEEP UNDERWATER! THEY RISE TO THE SURFACE TO BREATHE WITHOUT WAKING UP.

Hungry, Hungry Hippos

When the sun sets, hippos are ready to eat. These hungry animals eat for about six hours a night! As they **graze** in grasslands or forests, their strong lips help them bite plants. *CHOMP!* Hippos grind their food with flat teeth in the backs of their mouths. Then, their stomachs have three parts that break down the food the rest of the way.

HIPPOS CAN WANDER UP TO 20 MILES (32 KM) IN SEARCH OF PLANTS TO EAT.

Have You Herd?

ROAR! A hippo **herd** is noisy! Common hippos usually live in groups of 10 to 30 animals. Each herd includes **males** and **females**, but only one male is the leader.

A HIPPO HERD'S LEADER FLINGS POOP WITH HIS TAIL TO MARK HIS **TERRITORY**.

Male hippos sometimes fight over who's in charge. They open their mouths wide, swing their heads, and slash at each other with long teeth. Watch out!

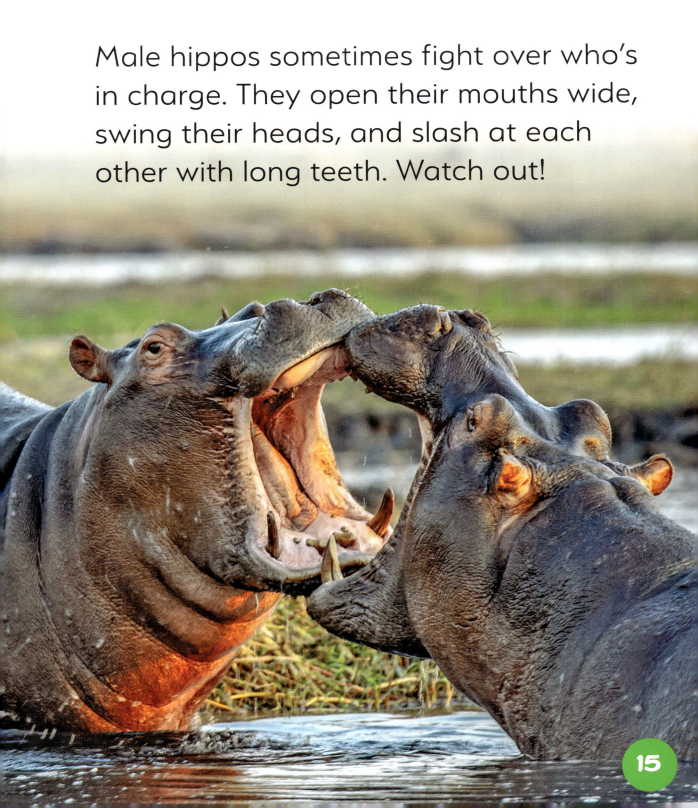

Harm to Hippos

Hippos may fight each other, but they don't need to fight off many **predators**. Most other animals leave these huge creatures alone. However, people are a danger to hippos and the lands where they live. Hunters kill the animals. Loggers cut down trees in their forest homes to get wood and make space for buildings. Farmers clear the land to grow crops.

PYGMY HIPPOS ARE **ENDANGERED**. THERE ARE FEWER THAN 3,000 OF THEM LEFT IN THE WILD.

It's Baby Time

A baby hippo, called a **calf**, is born seven to eight months after two adults **mate**. The mother leaves her herd to have the little hippo. She keeps the baby to herself until it grows stronger. Then, they rejoin the herd.

COMMON HIPPO MOTHERS USUALLY GIVE BIRTH IN WATER. PYGMY HIPPOS HAVE CALVES ON LAND.

Growing Up

Hippo calves grow fast! They drink milk from their mothers' bodies for several months. Soon, they start eating grasses, too.

At four years old, pygmy hippos are fully grown and ready to live on their own. Common hippos keep growing for several more years. When they are about seven years old, they can have their own young.

HIPPOS CAN LIVE FOR 30 TO 40 YEARS.

HIPPOPOTAMUSES ARE AWESOME!
LET'S LEARN EVEN MORE ABOUT THEM.

Kind of animal: Hippopotamuses are mammals. All mammals have hair or fur, give birth to live young, and drink milk from their mothers as babies.

Other hoofed mammals: Hippos are among the largest hoofed mammals. Rhinoceroses, giraffes, camels, and zebras are some others.

Size: Common hippos range in size from 10 to 16 feet (3 to 5 m) long. That's almost as long as a pickup truck. Pygmy hippos are about 5 ft (1.5 m) long—only as big as a park bench.

HIPPOS AROUND THE WORLD

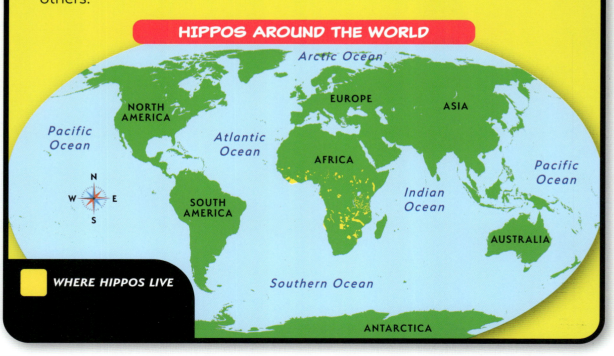

Arctic Ocean

EUROPE

ASIA

NORTH AMERICA

Pacific Ocean

Atlantic Ocean

AFRICA

Indian Ocean

Pacific Ocean

SOUTH AMERICA

AUSTRALIA

Southern Ocean

ANTARCTICA

N W E S

WHERE HIPPOS LIVE

Glossary

calf a baby hippo

endangered in danger of dying out completely

females hippos that can give birth to young

graze to eat grasses

herd a large group of animals that live together

hooves tough coverings that protect an animal's toes

males hippos that cannot give birth to young

mate to come together to have young

nostrils the two openings in a nose used for breathing and smelling

predators animals that hunt and kill other animals for food

territory the area where an animal lives

webbed connected by thin skin

Index

Read More

Downs, Kieran. *Nile Crocodile vs. Hippopotamus (Torque: Animal Battles).* Minneapolis: Bellwether Media, 2022.

Markovics, Joyce L. *Pygmy Hippos (On the Trail: Studying Secretive Animals in the Wild).* Ann Arbor, MI: Cherry Lake Publishing, 2021.

Learn More Online

1. Go to **www.factsurfer.com** or scan the QR code below.
2. Enter "**Hippopotamus**" into the search box.
3. Click on the cover of this book to see a list of websites.

About the Author

Colleen Sexton is a writer and editor. She is the author of more than 100 nonfiction books for kids on topics ranging from astronauts to glaciers to sharks. She lives in Minnesota.